From Milngavie to Midges

Hiking the West Highland way, Scotland

by
Paul Bissett

For my wife, Tracey, who was always first to the top of every hill.

"Where you lead, I will follow."

Contents

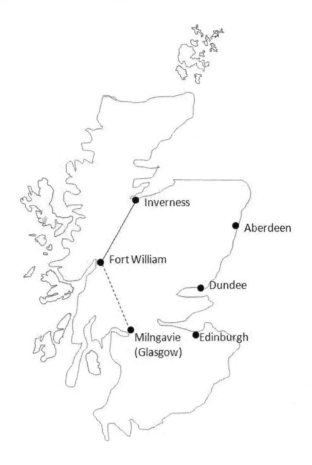

The dotted line denotes the West Highland Way from Milngavie on the outskirts of Glasgow to Fort William. The solid line denotes the Great Glen Way, from Fort William to Inverness. Not their exact routes, but a general guide in relation to the country as a whole.

"What do I know?"

I was born in Edinburgh and grew up camping and wandering around the countryside of Scotland. I went on my first organized hike in the Scottish mountains in 1975, courtesy of the British Royal Navy, later on in my naval career I took a mountain leaders course. This allowed me to teach map and compass skills, plan and lead expeditions up to the snow line anywhere in the world.

Over the years I put together many trips; planned routes, organizing the transport to and from the mountains, the accommodations, food, clothing and equipment. These trips included a number of "West Highland Way" hikes, and after its establishment the "Great Glen Way." I have hiked extensively on Dartmoor and Bodmin Moor in South West England as well as the lake district in North West England, I have also hiked in both the Brecon Beacons and Snowdonia national parks in Wales.

Although I'm loathe to admit it, as it tends to be looked down on by a certain section of outdoors people, I was probably a "Munro Bagger," (a mountain over 3,000 ft, which some people set out to collect or "bag" to the exclusion of all else) I bagged 77 before I left for distant shores.

In addition to many long distance hikes, I have done numerous day hikes all over the world, so have a good idea of what is required (and what isn't) for a fun and comfortable trip.

So you're going hiking in Scotland? Then there is probably a good chance that you will try a wee dram of scotch whisky while you are here or possibly even visit a distillery.

I do reference distilleries that are close to the trail in this book and my new book "Whisky Traveler" lists over 1000 whisky bars in 63 countries, many of them in Scotland. Just one thing, you should know, they don't call it "Scotch" in Scotland, they just ask for a whisky, or ask for it by specific brand.

In my biography at the end of the book, I have supplied my email and website, so, should you wish to discuss one of these hikes, you can contact me, (I am also happy to talk at length on the phone) if you'd prefer, just email me first to set up the call.

Chapter 1

Planning
(Where, when, why, how and who with?)

Although this book is about the "West Highland Way", I should mention that the "West Highland" and "Great Glen Ways" geographically speaking are one continuous trail from Milngavie (Mulguy) in the South to Inverness in the North.

Having said that, most people do them separately, mainly because of the distance, but also because of the time and cost involved. The total distance combined would be 269 kilometers or 168 miles depending on what currency your converting from. As to time and cost, obviously that comes down to how fit you are, how much holiday/vacation time you have and whether you plan on carrying your accommodation with you or sleeping in a hotel each night.

My preference is to do the hikes separately, as I have done previously, not because of a lack of fitness, when I was younger I completed a 101 mile hike, non-stop in 42 hours.

Nice to brag about over a couple of beers or whiskies with your buddies, but truth to tell, not that much fun.

Pushing yourself to your limits does, have its own rewards and if that's your thing, good for you, I get it. As I have aged (and gained experience) I have come to realize that my need to prove myself has diminished as measured against; stopping to take in the views, letting someone else carry my pack and sleeping in a comfortable bed each night.

I believe that's called wisdom, but I fought against it for a long time and it took my wife Tracey and our friend David McDonald to get me to relent on my need for self flagellation. I have now been converted to the dark side, and as I relax between clean sheets after a hot shower, a fine meal and a couple of drinks, call me shallow, but I don't really miss sleeping under canvas or getting eaten by midges*.

*As you would expect from the country that brought you "Nessie" the loch Ness monster, the Highland midge" has taken on an almost mythical status. I have heard it described as being about the size of a period (full stop) at the end of a sentence, with the teeth of an alligator. First things first, midges do not transmit diseases to humans, about the only thing transmitted will be the tall tales that you'll tell when you return home. The "midgie" as it is known in Scotland is so small that if you are walking, the wind of your passing will stop it from landing on you.
If there is a slight breeze you are safe, in fact about the only time that you are likely to get bitten is while asleep.

Mainly if you are camping, almost every hotel in the highlands of Scotland will have a warning about keeping your windows closed, because of the midges.

After all that, the bite doesn't hurt it just itches. You can use any insect repellant that would work for mosquitoes to keep them at bay or the old traditional method is to crush bog myrtle leaves in your palms and rub it on the exposed areas of skin. Which I have done to good effect in the past.

Bog Myrtle

Back to the hike; Your first two decisions are which hike and who do I hike with? Of the two, the second is the most important, I have found over numerous hikes and stressful situations that the military put me through, that people's true nature will out, when put under stress. If you haven't been in this sort of situation, you will probably blow that comment off and think no more about it.

My reason for mentioning it is, when your friends or loved ones get tired, and these hikes will make them tired, along with the possible aches and blisters that may occur, be prepared for cranky outbursts, they do happen.

Once the decision of who and where have been decided, we come to when? If you are planning on staying in hotels on the hike you need to book them almost a year in advance, as there are a limited number available to you. If you are planning on camping, there a campsites throughout the hikes, but these also fill up, so early booking doesn't hurt. To know which hotels or campsites you want, you need to work out how much distance you wish to cover each day.

For instance we did the following;

95 Miles from Milngavie to Ft. William

–   Day 1 Milngavie to Balmaha; 20 Miles

–   Day 2 Balmaha to Rowardennan; 7 Miles

–   Day 3 Rowardennan to Inverarnan; 14
     Miles

–   Day 4 Inverarnan to Bridge of Orchy; 19
     Miles

–   Day 5 Bridge of Orchy to Kinlochleven; 21
     Miles

–   Day 6 Kinlochleven to Fort William; 14
     Miles

Now you know your start and finish points each day, you can
book your accommodations. There are itineraries/distances
for 7, 8 and 9 day hikes at the end of chapter 2.

You should also allow enough time to work on your fitness,
being fit enough to play sports like football (soccer), or other
team games, or even running marathons (although that is
seriously fit), does not necessarily mean you can hike 100
miles comfortably.

Unlike team sports, that are played on nice surfaces and are
over after an hour or two, this is walking over rough ground for
six or more hours each day for a week or so, the distance and
rough ground accumulate to tire you more than you would
think. You are also using different muscle groups than you

use in other sports, so train for your hike, walk each day to get your body used to the constant exercise.

Now I have sown some doubts about hiking these long distance routes, let me reassure you. Almost 100,000 people hike the West Highland Way each year; all I'm trying to do is have you prepare yourself, so your hike is enjoyable.

Another reason to start training early is to make sure that your footwear is broken in and comfortable. The "West Highland Way" is hiked on some old military roads, that were constructed of stones and gravel.

A lot of the gravel has washed away over the centuries and exposed small embedded rocks that no matter how you try and avoid them, will, over the duration of the hike tenderize and bruise the soles of your feet, if you do not have good thick soles on your boots. I know this from experience, every hike except for the last "West Highland Way", was hiked in proper hiking boots with thick Vibram soles and I had no foot problems. The last WHW hike was in hiking shoes that were lighter with thinner soles and by the end of the hike my feet were so sore I could hardly walk.

Hiking boots with thick Vibram soles are less of a requirement on the "Great Glen Way" as the trail under foot is much more forgiving.

Having said that, I would always recommend proper hiking boots, as they also give great ankle support.

So far; You know which hike, you know who with, now you have to pick when? Traditionally April and September are the two months that have the least rainfall. My preference is for September as it is warmer and the ground is dryer. Also in September the heather should be in bloom, turning some of the hills purple, and the autumnal colors of the leaves makes for some wonderful photo opportunities.

No matter what time of year you hike either trail, you will likely get rained on, so you will need to carry (or wear) waterproof clothing. More on clothing choices in Chapter 4 – Resources.

Now let's look at what you don't need, you don't need a GPS, the entire route is way marked with posts with a thistle embossed into it, and if there is a fork in the trail there will be an arrow pointing you in the right direction.

Way Marker.

All you have to do is pay attention, you can get a map if you wish and I have, on both the WHW and GGW hikes, although not really necessary to stop you from getting lost. I like them for the information they give and to get a better perspective of the area you are hiking through. The maps I used, are the footprint maps which you can order online or wait until you get to your start point, you'll find them readily available in local shops. My own preference is to get them in advance.

Chapter 2

The overall hike

Scotland's first (and most popular) long distance route from;

Milngavie to Fort William

Distance: 95mi/151km

Duration: Your choice

Height Gain: 2,650ft/800m

The night prior to the hike – Milngavie

Travel Inn
West Highland Gate
103 Main Street
Milngavie
G62 6JJ

Day one

Milngavie to Balmaha

Distance: 19mi/31km

Duration: 5 to 6 hours

Height Gain: 984ft/300m

Ancestral lands of clan

Cunningham

Motto - "Over fork over"

Each morning at breakfast, I told my fellow travelers what clan lands we would be hiking through and any sights to look out for on the days hike.

After eighteen months of anticipation the hike starts (after walking a mile from our hotel) with a photo opportunity at the Obelisk in Milngavie Main Street. Heading North/West, out of town, the trail goes though parkland, open fields and follows a disused railway, with no major climbs. This is a relatively easy day's hike through fields and latterly forest, this is why I prefer to hike from Milngavie to Fort William, rather than North to South, the hike gets progressively harder as you head north, so your body (and mind) get used to the exertion as you head North.

Another consideration for starting in Milngavie is the weather, you are likely to get rain at some point on the hike, and the prevailing wind is usually from the South West, which would have it generally blowing from behind you and over your left shoulder as opposed to blowing in your face if you start the hike in Fort William.

We deliberately started a little late (9:30am) as I remembered (from previous hikes) that there was a Whisky Distillery (Glengoyne) about 30 minutes walk from the start. I had suggested to David and Tracey that we take one of the tours that started at 10am.

For the next three and a half hours I kept saying it must be just over the next hill or around the next bend, when we finally reached the Distillery, it would have involved climbing over a couple of fences and walking through a herd of cattle for about a quarter of a mile, we all agreed that it was not worth the effort.

We stopped for lunch at the Beech Tree Inn, where we sampled the Glengoyne 10-year-old Whisky, and concluded we had made the right choice not to visit the Distillery. In retrospect, having gained a greater understanding of whisky and having tasted the full Glengoyne range of whiskies, that conclusion was wrong. I can recommend visiting the distillery, as we went back and did so a few years later.

So far, the trail has been through undulating (hilly) parkland, woods and fields, most of the remainder of the day's walk would be along quiet country roads, until we reached the Queen Elizabeth National Forest, which would have been more scenic had not major logging been going on. This logging caused the first of our detours; We had planned to cross over Conic hill as the views from the summit, of Loch Lomond and the mountains behind are breathtaking, and if you have not hiked this trail before, quiet surprising.

Unfortunately the way ahead was closed, so we headed down to Drymen (Drim-en), a long and at this point in the days hike, hard descent.

This detour fortunately took us straight to the Clachan Inn (Licensed 1734) www.clachaninndrymen.co.uk, reputed to have been managed by the sister of the famous Scottish outlaw Rob Roy. Prior to the hike, I had read about the Heather Ale they served in the Clachan, unfortunately they had stopped serving it some years before. Still, they did have other beers that we could have, so we dropped our packs and sat down to enjoy a well earned drink. The bar was full of well dressed, lively men, both young and old, and judging by the flowers in the button holes of their jackets it was a wedding party. A short while later an older woman (equally well dressed) came into the bar and shouted at the men, something that we didn't understand (but they certainly did), they put down their drinks and left. After relaxing with a beer we took a taxi to our first nights lodging at the Oak Tree Inn, Balmaha, on the shores of Loch Lomond.

Time for a well deserved beer.

Possible Side trip

Glengoyne Distillery Founded 1833
www.glengoyne.com
An easy to visit distillery, just over a dozen miles from the
centre of Glasgow, six or seven from Loch Lomond, and a
quarter mile from the WHW trail. It is said that Rob Roy
McGregor hid in an oak tree just a few hundred yards from the
distillery.

1st night – Balmaha

The Oak Tree Inn
Balmaha
Loch Lomond G63 0JQ
www.theoaktreeinn.co.uk

Day Two

Balmaha to Rowardennan

Distance: 7mi/11km

Duration: 2 to 3 hours

Height Gain: 627ft/191m

Ancestral lands of clans

Buchanan
"Clarior hinc honos"
"Brighter hence the honor"

&

Graham
"Ne oublie"
"Do not forget"

My bad memory about how far it was to the Distillery and the length of the first days walk, seemed to have made my fellow hikers a little wary of any of my predictions for the rest of the hike.

The accommodations (overlooking Loch Lomond), the food, whisky selection and the people at the Oak Tree Inn are all to be recommended. We left the next morning around 9am with a packed lunch purchased from the Inn. Crossing the road and into a car park we stopped to take a photo by a sign that showed the Balmaha Millennium trail, at which point we were spotted by a lady from Tennessee.
She was obviously excited and we correctly assumed it was because we were wearing kilts, as she approached, I turned to David and said "leave the talking to me." I was born and raised in Scotland, David in America. Sure enough the nice lady wanted her picture taken with a couple of highlanders, and we were happy to oblige.

All of us were thankful that today was a short day, after way too many miles yesterday, it was also a lot more scenic than yesterday as we would spend all of today's hike on the Shores of Loch Lomond.

Today's hike was mostly up and down small hills with an occasional break to walk along a beach, we stopped and spoke with a couple that were training their Newfoundland's as water rescue dogs in the Loch.

A little further on we came across some hung-over young men that had, by all appearances had a great night. They were carrying the remnants of last night's reverie back out along the trail and insisted we take a beer apiece to lighten their load. We are nothing if not considerate, and did so.

Tracey drinking both hers and most of mine as I was struggling to breathe climbing the hills, so couldn't manage the beer drinking as well. At this time I should clarify, that I was carrying both my gear and Tracey's, a pack weighing around 50/60 lbs.

Free beer.

After a photo opportunity with some long red haired highland cows (Heilan coos, as the locals call them), we stopped at the edge of Loch Lomond and had a picnic with the lunch packed by the Oak Tree Inn.

I can't say that the packed lunch, lived up to the rest of our experience at the Oak Tree in, the sandwich had a thin slice of Ham on plain white bread which was tasteless.
Fortunately the surroundings saved the picnic, a more spectacular place to stop for lunch would be hard to find.

Our days hike came to a surprising and fortunately quick end as the Rowardennan Hotel (Circa. 1696) came into view, I say fortunately as yesterdays hike was still fresh in our memories and our legs.

The Rowardennan Hotel sits at the end of the road, on the South side of Loch Lomond (no more cars), under the most southerly Munro (Ben Lomond) in Scotland, right on the edge of Loch Lomond a beautiful setting.

The three of us made our way to the bar after bathing and changing, I point out the obvious here in case anyone is thinking of carrying a tent and camping out. Go with a hotel for each night, they are ideally spaced along the way. I have done both on this hike and the luxury of a real bed and a shower/bath is well worth the extra expense.

We ate dinner, sat at the Bar and spent time talking with the bartender Danny, who even for me was hard to decipher.

As yesterday, at the Oak Tree Inn the staff were a mix of Scots and young people from around the world, Canada, England and South Africa were represented.

The bar had a mix of hikers and locals, after David had gone to bed Tracey and I talked for a while with a nice couple, who invited us to go for a sail on their boat on loch Lomond with them if we ever came through here again.

On going to bed we saw a sign by the windows, warning us against opening the windows as the Highland midgie would come in and eat us alive, this sign was too been seen in all our hotels along the way.

Possible Side trip

Hiking to the top of Ben Lomond, (the views are breathtakingly spectacular. **7.5 miles/4.5 to 5 hours**

Start from the car park at Rowardennan where there is an information centre and toilets. The mountain is not in view from the car park but can be seen from the metal jetty on the loch shore. The ascent starts from a clearly marked path at the back of the information building. A good reference for this hike is the Walk highlands website.
http://www.walkhighlands.co.uk/lochlomond/ben-lomond.shtml

2nd night – Rowardennan

Rowardennan Hotel
Loch Lomond
Scotland
G63 0AR
www.rowardennanhotel.co.uk

Day Three

Rowardennan to Inverarnan

Distance: 14mi/22km

Duration: 6 to 7 hours

Height Gain: 1558ft/475m

Ancestral lands of clan

McGregor

"S rioghal mo dhream"
"Royal is my race"

In the forest

When we woke in the morning it was raining, our first thought was to build an ark, the word torrential came to mind, well it is Scotland after all. This is where Tracey showed how much smarter than me she is, David and I had been carrying large rucksacks with all our clothes for the trip.

Tracey said she had seen leaflets in each of the hotels for a portage service to take our bags on to the next hotel, and that we should use it. Call me lazy if you want, but to me that was inspiration, the rest of the hike was so much more enjoyable.

After yet another Scottish breakfast consisting of Sausage, Bacon, Eggs, Black Pudding, Beans, Tomato and toast (also cereal if you want it).

We donned our wet weather gear including our high tech kilt covers (Black plastic trash bags, which led to my search for proper kilt covers on our return home). Today's hike was again along the shore of Loch Lomond, mainly through forest, as we set off, the rain continued to pour down. After a short distance the roads disappeared and the trail grew steadily narrower as we appeared to go back in time.

Tracey's comment on the trail was "the forest primeval" and later she said it was like walking to Rivendell, from the Lord of the Rings trilogy, which elicited comments later of "Frodo do you think we'll ever see the Shire again?" and "come on Frodo keep up."

We lost count of the streams that we had to cross that were overflowing their banks from the water running off Ben Lomond.

There were a huge number of waterfalls along this section of the trail as we hiked through the old wood with an otherworldly feel to it.

We stopped at the Inversnaid Hotel for lunch (a favorite vacation spot of Queen Victoria and on the subject of Queen Victoria; she did not approve of women smoking, but when on her trips to the highlands she frequently smoked to keep the midges at bay), this is the site of the home of Rob Roy MacGregor, when he briefly held the title Laird (lord) of Inversnaid.

After lunch we carried on and the path got rougher, we soon passed 'Rob Roy's Cave' where he supposedly held hostages for ransom. Having just hiked through the area I can see why he chose it, a more remote and difficult spot to traverse would be hard to find anywhere in the surrounding land.

We eventually saw the end of Loch Lomond through the mist, and the rain had finally relented as we came upon a Bothy* with smoke coming out of the chimney.

We went inside and there were the two young men whom we had talked to earlier on the trail, they were spending the night here.

We left the young men to their Bothy (in the photo below), all the while thankful that our next hotel came with Jacuzzi tubs. About an hour later we arrived at the Drovers inn (Est. 1705), the Inn looked like it had not been renovated since 1705. Our accommodation however was across the road and relatively new, after availing ourselves of the Jacuzzi tub we met David in the bar.

Where whisky, beer and Highlander Burgers (cheeseburger with haggis on top) for Dinner, was the order of the day. Although the inn seemed a little careworn, the bar was overflowing with people having a great time and to add a little local color the two young men tending bar were wearing kilts. When I asked what clans the tartan represented neither of them knew, it turns out that one of them was English and the other South African.

*Personally this was my least favorite place to stay, compared to our other accommodations, the hotel could do with a makeover (not our rooms over the road), and the staff here were acceptable, but not overly friendly. To be fair to the staff the hotel was very busy, and there was a good atmosphere in the bar and the real peat+ fire was a nice touch.

*The Drover's Inn has since had a makeover and I would stay there again.

* Bothy - a small hut (the one on far the right) previously used by shepherds, now open for anyone to use Bothy's can be found throughout the Scottish highlands, they usually consist (as this one did) of four walls, a roof, boarded up windows, and a door, there is no furniture, but usually there is a stock of firewood and of course the most important thing if you're young and on tight budget, it's free.

+ Peat - a brown, soil-like material cut from boggy ground, consisting of partly decomposed vegetable matter. It is widely cut and dried for use in gardening and as a fuel.

3rd night – Inverarnan

The Drovers Inn
Inverarnan by Ardlui
North Loch Lomond
G83 7DX I
www.droversinn.co.uk

Day four

Inverarnan to Bridge or Orchy

Distance: 19mi/31km

Duration: 6 to 7 hours

Height Gain: 2560ft/780m

Ancestral lands of clan

Campbell

"Ne Obliviscaris"
"Forget not"

Leaving the Drovers Inn, we stopped at Beinglas farm shop and bought Tracey and myself a hiking pole each and a small day rucksack for myself. We continued north along Glen Falloch. The scenery is beautiful and the walk to Crianlarich (cry-an-larick) is easy, if you like walking uphill. After leaving Inverarnan the Glen starts to open up and the mountains drawback, allowing us to see farther, the scenery is entirely different from the old forest we hiked through yesterday.

At some point, due to looking at the scenery and talking too much, we missed one of the trail markers and ended up off the trail and walking on the road, but still headed in the right direction.
After a short distance we could see the trail about half a mile to the right, but we were on the wrong side of the river Falloch. Our navigational error did bring us some joy; we came across the falls of Falloch, very scenic.
Shortly after the falls, we found a way back over to the trail, the trail is like Scotland in miniature, with rocks sticking up like small mountains, not at all comfortable. This is the old 18th century military road built by General Wade to help the government control the highlanders.

Extract taken from a Canadian hiker's diary;
"During the day, I began to overtake groups from the Dutch army that were walking the West Highland Way as a training exercise. Over the next few days, I learned that they were all medics and that the party of 48 was camping at night and travelling in groups of 6 or 7 people. They had helped a number of walkers with various walking ailments. By the end of the walk they had lost five of their own people to knee and foot problems and another to a broken leg. I could see about half the rest of them were limping."

Today like every other day, a hill climbing day, in forests and out, the rain has come and gone, and being a nineteen mile day the trail seems to go on forever. We have been hiking on the West side of the Glen all day, we now come down out of the forest (again) and cross the A82, and through a field to the Kirkton bridge which spans the Fillian river, shortly to pass the ruins of St. Fillian's Chapel and onwards for lunch at the Auchtertyre (Ok-ter-tire) farm shop.

As we leave it's raining again, we re-cross the A82 about half a mile further on, I realize I've left my hiking stick at the farm shop, and return to get it (always check you have everything after a stop), we now join the path that follows the river Cononish to the village of Tyndrum.

This is where Tracey finally admitted that she was in a great deal of pain, I looked at her feet and she had blisters the size of grapes on the little toe of both feet. We sat outside the village shop and I dressed them for her, but she could not get her walking shoes back on, this is the point where her hike ended (temporarily), she caught a taxi to the hotel at Bridge of Orchy about five miles farther on.

David and I marched on along what initially was a good surfaced old military road, which later turned into, something that looked like a landslide down the side of the mountain. We kept at it and eventually made it to the Bridge of Orchy hotel. This was, the best hotel so far, the accommodations and food were top notch and the staff very friendly, it was also the most expensive. Go figure! The best hotel was the most expensive?

Quick march.

They have a nice deck built on the outside of the hotel, just off the bar that faces the river Orchy. So after dinner we thought we would go and sit outside and take in the views, but the midges were waiting for their dinner, so we decided against it.

Possible Side trip

Hike Beinn Dorain, quite steep, but again stunning views to be had. If you are lucky, you might, as I did, get to see the Royal Air Force pilots fly their jets beneath you through the glen.
8.75 miles/6 to 8 hours

A good reference for this hike is the Walk highlands website.
http://www.walkhighlands.co.uk/lochlomond/ben-lomond.shtml

4th night - Bridge of Orchy

Bridge of Orchy Hotel
Bridge of Orchy
Argyll, PA 36 4AD
www.bridgeoforchy.co.uk

Day five

Bridge of Orchy to Kinlochleven

Distance: 21mi/34km

Duration: 6 to 8 hours

Height Gain: 2440ft/744m

Ancestral lands of clans

Campbell
"Ne Obliviscaris"
"Forget not"

&

Donald
"Per mare, Per terras"
"By sea and by land"

We had yet another full cooked Scottish breakfast, then I said my farewells to Tracey, her blistered feet were in no condition to take on Rannoch Moor.
David and I set off by crossing the River Orchy, over the Bridge of the same name (built 1753), we were in for a long day after yesterdays 19 miles, as we had 21 miles to do today.

Two miles after leaving Bridge of Orchy you come to Inveroran, which consists of a couple of houses and a hotel, thereafter the Way goes up an old Drover/military road, peaking out at just over 300m, and giving open wonderful views over the Blackmount Forest, just above the trail is a stone marker where Ian Fleming's (Author of James Bond) brother died while out Stag hunting, from Ian's estate. We were now on Rannoch Moor, the largest uninhabited wilderness in the UK, this was the worst area for bugs on the whole hike, large horse flies kept landing on our unprotected legs and biting, bug spray would have been good.

As you continue on Buachaille Etive Mòr, (Book-ale-etive-mor - the great Shepherd of Glen Etive) comes into view standing guard over the entrance to both Glen Etive and Glencoe. Our lunchtime destination (the Kingshouse Inn) and our rendezvous with Tracey comes into view, although still a few miles away.

After a lunch of hot soup, bread and spectacular views, we say farewell to Tracey and set off for the hour's hike to the foot of the Devil's staircase, surprise, surprise it's raining again. It takes a further hour of steady climbing to reach the top, it's during this zigzag climb that we find out how cunning the *"Highland Midgie"* can be, while you are moving they can't get you, so they wait for you to stop to catch your breath then pounce and the feeding frenzy begins.

David and I stopped at the top of the Devil's staircase for a photo or two; we were safe from the Midges here as there was a slight breeze. David said "you don't look too happy Paul", I replied, "I know what's coming." We now faced a three hour downhill hike to Kinlochleven over some very bad trails (not fun).

The countryside is very bleak on the North of the Devil's Staircase – no houses and not even a sheep in sight. Shortly afterwards the depression factor kicked in, we could see Kinlochleven in the distance, the end of today's hike, unfortunately the trail would veer away to contour around a mountain and lose sight of it, then it would reappear, this happens a number of times, which does get frustrating.

When we finally made it into Kinlochleven we were passing a campsite when a young Girl saw us and started shouting in French and running around looking for something, it turned out to be her camera, she wanted her picture taken with men in kilts, we are now in an album in France.

Shortly after we arrived at the Tailrace Inn, where I ordered a beer and David had a Glenmorangie (now that he could pronounce it), while we waited for a Taxi to take us to our accommodations in Glencoe. There are many accommodation options available in Kinlochleven, I stayed in a good bunkhouse on some of my previous hikes and camped in the Lairigmor above Kinlochlven on others, there are also hotels to be had. We had chosen to stay in Glencoe as David McDonald wanted to stay where his ancestors were from.

Possible Side trips

The films/movies "Highlander" and "Highlander 3"
Were partially shot in Glencoe.

The Harry Potter films/movies
Were partially shot (Hagrid's hut) in Glencoe.

Glencoe visitor center
www.visitscotland.com/info/see-do/glencoe-visitor-centre-p247481

Glencoe massacre monument
www.glencoescotland.com/about-glencoe/history
We took this side trip, as outlined in the next chapter.

5th night - Glencoe

The Clachaig Inn
Clachaig,
Glencoe,
Argyll, Scotland
PH49 4HX

https://clachaig.com

Day six

Kinlochleven to Fort William

Distance: 14mi/23km

Duration: 5 to 7 hours

Height Gain: 1558ft/475m

Ancestral lands of clans

Donald
"Permare, Per terras"
"By sea and by land"

&

Cameron
"Aonaibh Ri Chéile,"
"Let Us Unite."

Yes, you can get too much of a good thing; the standard, huge cooked Scottish breakfast was for me, starting to get a bit much, although it does stand you in good stead for the days hike. Outside we meet up again with Kenny our taxi driver from yesterday. Kenny was going to take us for a drive through Glencoe before taking us back to Kinlochleven to continue our hike.

Kenny turned out to be a bit of a tour guide as well as a taxi driver, he gave us a running commentary as we made our way up and then back down Glencoe. He suggested we stop at the Glencoe visitor center, which we did and saw some of the history of the Glen, he then took us to the Monument in Glencoe village that commemorates the massacre, he also pointed out a park and explained that it was made for the wife of a MacDonald who had gone to America and married a native American. He brought her back to Glencoe and had the park made for her, with trees and shrubs from America, so she would not feel homesick.

We made our way back to the trail in Kinlochleven, according to the guidebooks, the Way starts with a "stiff" climb from sea level. Despite several breathers on the way up, in my opinion, this "stiff" climb is harder than the Devil's Staircase!

Top of the climb out of Kinlochleven.

As we came out above the tree line, we rejoined the old military road at the top of the climb. We then hiked for 5 miles through the Lairigmor – a long deserted glen with only two ruined farms as evidence of previous human occupation.

The Lairigmor runs parallel to Loch Leven, but you would not know that, as the glen is hidden in the hills. As we approached the first of the ruined farms we saw a small group of people and one of the women started doing the by now familiar *"look there are men in kilts dance"* as she tried to find her camera.

We posed with her and are now in an album in Switzerland.

Turning north, the path leaves the old military road at around 7.5 miles. Here there is an option to follow the forest trail or follow the country roads into Fort William, we set off on the forest trail, but after a short way, we stopped and discussed our options again.

The forest was more like a wasteland as far ahead as we could see, there were major logging operation going on.

We turned back to the junction and set off on the country roads, which was very scenic, in fact Tracey said that she would quite like to live in the area we were walking through, a word of warning, this route is very hilly (same old, same old). We came up yet another hill and without any warning there nestled below us was Fort William, sitting on Loch Linnhe the deepest loch in Scotland.

Our long descent into Fort William, then along through the main street on aching and blistered feet was finally topped off with exultant photos taken at the large Thistle shaped sign *"End of the West Highland Way."*

End of hike comments;
Tracey "We're here, we're here, thank god we're here"
David "Quick take my picture before I die."

David, Tracey and myself

Fortunately our hotel for the evening was only a few hundred yards away, and when we got there they gave us a much needed shot of single malt whisky, it would have tasted heavenly anyway, but the fact it was free and drank at the end of our almost 100 mile hike made it all the better.

Possible Side trips around Fort William

Hike to the top of Ben Nevis, the highest mountain in Scotland (and Britain). I wouldn't recommend this after a hike, but prior (the day before) to the hike, if you start here in Fort William. Take the tourist trail to the top, for a relatively easy ascent, if the weather is clear the views are fantastic.
Glen Nevis, a 15 minute drive, followed by a short walk through an beautiful alpine gorge, whose boulders have been carved by the rushing snow melt. As you come out of the narrow gorge, Glen Nevis opens up in front of you and on your right is "Steal falls" with a 3 wire rope bridge if you're feeling acrobatic.

Ben Nevis distillery - Established in 1825, Ben Nevis is one of the oldest distilleries in Scotland. Incorporated within the visitor center (built into an old warehouse dating from 1862) is "The Legend of the Dew of Ben Nevis" in which you will meet the giant "Hector McDram" who will tell of the legend of the Dew.
www.bennevisdistillery.com

Outdoors; Sea kayaking, white water rafting, rock climbing, mountain biking, skiing (in winter) and just about anything to do with outdoor fun.

Harry Potter fan? The Hogwarts express (real name "The Jacobite"), runs from Fort William to Mallaig and back, passing over the Glenfinnan viaduct. Which I'm sure you will remember as that was where the train almost collided with the flying car with Harry and Ron in it.

I believe the underpass close to Nevis sports store was used in one of the Harry Potter films, for the scene where Harry and his cousin Dudley are attacked by Dementors.

"Braveheart" although most of the filming took place in Ireland. The village scenes of William Wallace as a child and again as a man returning back home, were filmed in Glen Nevis.

"Highlander" and "Highlander 3"
Were partially shot in Glen Nevis.

"Rob Roy" just a few weeks after the "Braveheart" crew left Glen Nevis the "Rob Roy" crew arrived with Liam Neeson to start filming.

Shopping Almost anything you could want, will be found on the main street of Fort William, from Outdoor clothing to Whisky.

7th night – Fort William

Distillery Guest House
Nevis Bridge, North Road
Fort William PH33 6LR

Looking back on the hike (lessons learned)

In retrospect we should have done the hike over 8 or 9 days and not 6 days, we could have stopped in Drymen at the end of the first day and not skirted round and then been forced to divert back, due to logging.

Later in the hike we should have split the longer days in half as well, we could have cut out a lot of the pain and made the whole experience even more enjoyable. Taking longer to do the hikes also allows for side trips to do and see things that you would otherwise miss.

If you live in Scotland that may not be a big deal as you can easily come back, but if you live in another country, even with the best of intentions you may never get back and see those sights. So, in my opinion taking more days to do the hike just makes more sense.

Here are some options;

7 day hike

- Day 1 Milngavie to Balmaha; 20 Miles
- Day 2 Balmaha to Rowardennan; 7 Miles
- Day 3 Rowardennan to Inverarnan; 14 Miles
- Day 4 Inverarnan to Bridge or Orchy; 19 Miles
- Day 5 Bridge of Orchy to Kings house; 13 Miles
- Day 6 to Kings house to Kinlochleven; 8 Miles
- Day 7 Kinlochleven to Fort. William; 14 Miles

8 day hike

- Day 1 Milngavie to Drymen 12 miles
- Day 2 Drymen to Rowardennan 10 miles
- Day 3 Rowardennan to Inversnaid hotel 13 miles
- Day 4 Inversnaid hotel to Drover's inn 7 miles
- Day 5 Drover's inn to Bridge of Orchy 17.5 miles
- Day 6 Bridge of Orchy to King's house 12.5 miles
- Day 7 King's house to Kinlochleven 9 miles
- Day 8 Kinlochleven to Fort William 14 miles

9 day hike

- Day 1 Milngavie to Drymen 12 miles
- Day 2 Drymen to Rowardennan 10 miles
- Day 3 Rowardennan to Inversnaid hotel 13 miles
- Day 4 Inversnaid hotel to Drover's inn 7 miles
- Day 5 Drover's inn to Crianlarich 6.5 miles
- Day 6 Crianlarich to Bridge of Orchy 11 miles
- Day 7 Bridge of Orchy to King's house 12.5 miles
- Day 8 King's house to Kinlochleven 9 miles
- Day 9 Kinlochleven to Fort William 14 miles

Good boots with a thick sole are essential, Tracey and I had walking shoes and David had good walking boots, he did not get blistered or bruised soles, and we got both. A Gore-Tex (or any waterproof) jacket is a much better idea than cheap plastic Ponchos that blow around in the wind and let the rain in, as well as acting like a sauna, they also rip easily and the fasteners keep popping open.

If wearing a kilt, spray your legs prior to starting each day with a bug spray.

Have your stuff ported on to the next hotel; just carry a day bag for your lunch/snacks and water.

Ensure you have a good blister kit, just in case.

Make sure you have some cash on you as occasionally you may come across a little shop where you can grab a snack or a souvenir.

Chapter 3

Other long distance trails in Scotland

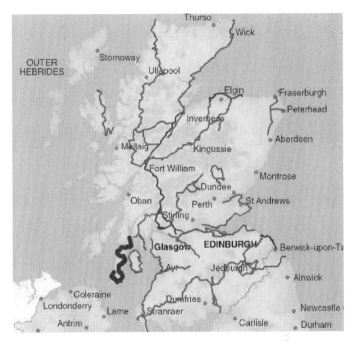

For the full interactive map and a wealth of information on hiking in Scotland go to www.walkhighlands.co.uk or you can go to any of the other referenced web sites. What follows is meant to whet your appetite for more hikes and point you to more comprehensive information.

Affric Kintail Way

From Drumnadrochit on the shores of Loch Ness, to Morvich in Kintail.
Distance: 44mi/71km
Duration: 5-10 days
Height Gain: 2640ft/ 800m
www.affrickintailway.com

Annandale Way

From the mouth of the River Annan and Solway Firth to Annandale Head in the hills north of the town of Moffat.
Distance: 55mi/ 88km
Duration: 5 days
Height Gain: 3780ft/ 1152m
http://annandaleway.org

Arran Coastal Way

A circuit around the isle of Arran.
Distance: 66mi/109km
Duration: 10 days
Height Gain: 6863ft/2092m*
*This is dependent on whether you take in Goatfell or any of the alternate routes or not.
www.coastalway.co.uk

Ayrshire Coastal Path
Follows the coastline for most of the hike with great views.
Distance: 100mi/150km
Duration: 5-10 days
Height Gain: 2640ft/800m
http://ayrshirecoastalpath.org

Berwickshire Coastal Path

As the name suggests, this trail follows the coast.
Distance: 30mi/48km
Duration: 2-4 days
Height Gain: 3280ft/1000m
https://walkscottishborders.com/route/berwickshire-coastal-path

Borders Abbeys Way
A circular hike connecting the historic Border towns and their famous Abbeys.
Distance: 64.4mi/103km
Duration: 4 days
Height Gain: 990ft/300m
www.bordersabbeysway.com

Cape Wrath Trail
The Cape Wrath Trail is a long distance walk from Fort William to the north western most point of mainland Britain, Cape Wrath. This is one for experienced hikers only, you will need to be competent with a map and compass, as the way is unmarked. you will also need to carry a tent and supplies for most of the way, you will be traversing rough ground and fording rivers. This is not a hike to do on a whim.
Distance: 235mi/378km
Duration: 14 to 18 days
Height Gain: 33543ft/10224m
https://capewrathtrailguide.org

Clyde Walkway
Distance: 40mi/65km
Duration: 5 days
Height Gain: 2355ft/718m
www.walkhighlands.co.uk

Cateran Trail
Named after local cattle rustlers, is a circular route from Blairgowrie.
Distance: 60mi/96km
Duration: 5 days
Height Gain: 3168ft/960m
www.walkthecaterantrail.com

Cowal Way
Takes you through Argyll's Cowal peninsula running from
Portavadie to Ardgartan.
Distance: 57mi/92km
Duration: 5 days
Height Gain: 5082ft/1540m
www.cowalway.co.uk

Dava Way
Looking at the distance, not that hard, but there is only
accommodation at either end, so you will need to take a tend
and supplies with you.
Distance: 23mi/38km
Duration: 1 to 3 days
Height Gain: 480ft/146m
www.walkhighlands.co.uk

East Highland Way
Partly way marked, partly wild hiking.
Distance: 80mi/128km
Duration: 4 to 7 days
Height Gain: 4622ft/1409m
www.easthighlandway.com

Fife Coastal Path
A relatively easy hike, with views over the river Forth to Edinburgh and the bridges.
Distance: 94mi/150km
Duration: 5 - 7 days
Height Gain: 330ft/100m
www.fifecoastalpath.co.uk

Formartine and Buchan Way
Aberdeen to Peterhead and Fraserburgh or vice-versa along an old railway.
Distance: 53mi/86km
Duration: 5 days
Height Gain: 660ft/200m
www.walkhighlands.co.uk

Forth & Clyde and Union Canals
Walking on towpaths, easy access to hotels, food and transport.
Distance: 63mi/101km
Duration: 3 to 4 days
Height Gain: 654ft/188m
www.walkhighlands.co.uk

John Muir Way

Coast to coast, crossing Scotland's heartland from Dunbar in the East to Helensburgh in the West

Distance: 134mi/215 km
Duration: 7-10 days
Height Gain: 330ft/100m

Yes, there is a John Muir way in Scotland as well as America, this is the route that he walked from his home in Dunbar across Scotland to Helensburgh to catch the boat to America. This route passes through the area I grew up in, some lovely coastal walks and castles to visit.
http://johnmuirway.org

John O'Groats Trail

This is not a formal trail, so there is little, to no way marking.

Distance: 146mi/235km
Duration: 14 days
Height Gain: 15206ft/4635m
www.walkhighlands.co.uk

Kelvin Way

Glasgow to Milngavie Although not a long distance path, you can start with this and join onto the West Highland Way at Milngavie. The Kelvin way runs from the centre of Glasgow, to Milngavie. The route mainly follows three rivers the Allander, Kelvin and Clyde.

Distance: 11 mi/17km
Duration: 5 hours
Height Gain: 548ft/167m
www.walkhighlands.co.uk

Kintyre Way
Traversing the Kintyre penninsuala.
Distance: 88mi/142km
Duration: 4-7 days
Height Gain: 1320ft/400m
I highly recommend staying at the Ardshiel hotel in Campbeltown (https://ardshiel.co.uk) if you hike this route. The food is superb, the whisky selection is huge (over 700).
www.kintyreway.com

Minigaig Pass
Recommended for experienced hikers only. From Blair Atholl to Kingussie.
Distance: 27mi/42km
Duration: 1-2 days
Height Gain: 3696ft/1120m
www.ldwa.org.uk

Moray Coast Trail
Paths and sandy beaches.
Distance: 45mi/72km
Duration: 3 to 5 days
Height Gain: 1345ft/410m
www.morayways.org.uk/moray-coast-trail.asp

Mull of Galloway trail
Paths and sandy beaches.
Distance: 45mi/72km
Duration: 3 days
Height Gain: 1345ft/410m
www.walkhighlands.co.uk

River Ayr Way
Glenbuck in East Ayrshire to the town of Ayr.
Distance: 41mi/66km
Duration: 2 to 4 days
Height Gain: 1540ft/469m
www.walkhighlands.co.uk

Rob Roy Way
The Rob Roy Way joins the town of Drymen to the Highland Perthshire town of Pitlochry.
Distance: 93mi/148km
Duration: 7 days
Height Gain: 1650ft/500m
www.robroyway.com

Scottish National Trail

Scotland's longest route, crossing Scotland from South to North or vice versa.

Extract from the walk Highlands website;

The Scottish National Trail is a challenging, 864 kilometre-long unofficial long distance walking route running the length of Scotland from Kirk Yetholm to Cape Wrath.

The route combines sections of official routes such as St Cuthbert's Way, the Southern Upland Way, the Forth and Clyde and Union Canals, the West Highland Way and the Rob Roy Way. Other parts - including sections through central Perthshire, the Cairngorms and the Northwest Highlands - make for a more serious backpacking route with neither way marking nor a continuous path, as well as a number of potentially hazardous river crossings.

Go to their website below for all the details.

Distance: 536mi/864km

Duration: 35 days

Height Gain: If you are willing to try this, then who cares about the height gain.

www.walkhighlands.co.uk

Skye Trail

Challenging, unofficial route for experienced hikers.

Distance: 80mi/128km

Duration: 7 days

Height Gain: 12404ft/3781m

www.walkhighlands.co.uk

Southern Upland Way

Used to be Scotland's longest route, crossing Scotland from coast-to-coast, until the National Trail (above) came along.
Distance: 212mi/340km
Duration: 12-20 days
Height Gain: 4785ft/1450m
www.southernuplandway.gov.uk

South Loch Ness Trail

From Fort Augustus to Inverness using the South side of the loch.
Distance: 36mi/58km
Duration: 3 days
Height Gain: 4461ft/1360m
www.walkhighlands.co.uk

Speyside Way

From Buckie on the Moray Coast to Aviemore in the Cairngorms, because it's easier walking down hill (South).
Distance: 65mi/105km
Duration: 4-7 days
Height Gain: 1650ft/500m
www.speysideway.org

St Cuthbert's Way
Connecting the Scottish border town of Melrose (and it's Abbey) with the holy island of Lindisfarne in England.
Distance: 62mi/100km
Duration: 4 days
Height Gain: 221ft/370m
www.stcuthbertsway.info

The Great Glen Way
Walking alongside lochs and through forests.
Distance: 79mi/127km
Duration: 5 to 7 days
Height Gain: 7253ft/2211m
www.highland.gov.uk/ggw

The West Highland Way
The West Highland Way was Scotland's first long distance route and is still the most popular. Stretching for 95 miles from Milngavie (Mulguy) on the edge of Glasgow to Fort William in the highlands.
Distance: 95mi/153km
Duration: 6 days
Height Gain: 9016ft/2748m
www.westhighlandway.org

Three Lochs Way
This way links Loch Lomond, Gare Loch and Loch Long.
Distance: 33mi/53km
Duration: 3 to 4 days
Height Gain: 3845ft/1172m
www.walkhighlands.co.uk

The West Island Way
This route takes you across the island of Bute.
Distance: 27mi/45km
Duration: 2 to 3 days
Height Gain: 3064ft/934m
www.walkhighlands.co.uk

Chapter 4

Resources/Tips/Tricks

Stops on the hike **"First-to-Last**

Banks
ATMs can be found in Milngavie, Kinlochleven and Fort William

Milngavie has;
Everything you could possibly need, apart from an airport.

Lots of accommodation
Restaurants & bars

Local Buses
Scottish City Link Tel: 0990 50 50 50
www.citylink.co.uk

National bus company
Stagecoach - www.stagecoachbus.com

ScotRail
National Rail Enquiries - 08457 484950
www.scotrail.co.uk

Balmaha has;

The oak Tree Inn
Accommodation, restaurant & bar
And it's own brewery
www.theoaktreeinn.co.uk

A Coffee shop & Ice cream parlour

Local Buses
www.carlberry.co.uk

A Village shop

Rowardennan has;

The Rowardennan hotel
Accommodation, restaurant & bar
www.rowardennanhotel.co.uk

Inversnaid Hotel
A great lunch stop, for us. I would like to go back and stay the night here.
www.lochsandglens.com/our-hotels/inversnaid-hotel

Inverarnan has;

The Drover's Inn
Accommodation, restaurant & bar
www.droversinn.co.uk

Beinglas farm
Accommodation, restaurant & bar
www.beinglascampsite.co.uk

Bridge of Orchy has;
Accommodation, restaurant & bar
www.bridgeoforchy.co.uk

Kinlochleven has;
Lots of Accommodation, Cafes/restaurant & bars
A supermarket

Fort William has;
Everything you could possibly need, apart from an airport.
www.visitfortwilliam.co.uk

Fort William Tourist Information Centre
email: fortwilliam@visitscotland.com

Car Hire
www.fortwilliamcarhire.com

www.easydrivescotland.co.uk

Local Buses
Scottish City Link Tel: 0990 50 50 50
www.citylink.co.uk

National bus company
Stagecoach www.stagecoachbus.com

ScotRail
National Rail Enquiries - 08457 484950
www.scotrail.co.uk

Baggage transfer companies
Pick up your baggage and deliver it to your next
accommodation each day, so you can hike unencumbered.
Cost per bag/rucksack will be around 40 to 50 British pounds
or 60 to 70 dollars for the whole way. I have no connection to
any of these companies.

A2B TRAVEL-LITE Est. 1995

Gilbert McVean
The Iron Chef,
5 Mugdock Road, Milngavie
G62 8PD

Contact Details:
Tel: +44(0)141 956 7890
Mobile/cell: +44(0)7778 966 592
http://travel-lite-uk.com
info@travel-lite-uk.com

A1- AMS SCOTLAND LIMITED Est. 2001

Bill Mitchell
22 Redhills View
Lennoxtown, Glasgow
G66 7BL

Contact Details:
Tel: +44(0)1360 312840
Mobile/cell: +44(0)787 282 3940
http://amsscotland.co.uk
info@amsscotland.co.uk

GINGER ROUTES

Cameron Farm
Alexandria
G83 8QZ

Contact Details:
Tel: 07577 463 613
http://www.gingerroutes.com
mail@gingerroutes.com

Accommodation information

With the ease of using the internet these days, finding accommodation should be relatively painless. I like to use Google maps and enter "hotels near" whichever place I wish to stay, that way I can see what's closest. I then click on the hotel icon and if it has a website, I look to see what the rooms, facilities and cost are like. You can then, if you wish, cross check with one of the websites listed under the useful websites heading later in this chapter, I like Trip Advisor as it lists the hotels as rated by the public.

I also give my thoughts on hotels I've stayed at on Trip advisor, I get nothing for doing it, so I'm OK with recommending it. Another consideration for accommodation is..............do you have to stay? For instance Milngavie is 40 minutes from Glasgow by train, so you could arrive in the morning and not spend the night prior to the hike in a hotel.

The same at the end of the hike there are good train and bus services in Fort William, so you could just leave when you finish. The same goes for Inverness, good transportation links. Now having said that, you're not going to be saving huge amounts of money. I would recommend arriving early, looking around, having dinner and a good night's sleep, and the same at the end of your hike.

Some accommodation websites

www.googlemaps.com

www.hotels.com

www.expedia.com

www.greatvaluevacations.com/hotels/europe/scotland/edinburgh/scotland-b-and-b-s-and-small-hotels

www.privatehousestays.com

www.scotlandsbestbandbs.co.uk

www.tripadvisor.com

www.trivago.com

www.visitscotland.com/accommodation

Equipment

There is obviously some crossover between what you need for the hike while staying in a hotel every night and camping each night. I don't know your personal needs, so this is a guide to what you'll need, not a definitive list.

Staying in Hotels

- Rucksacks/suitcases (your choice to port on or carry)
- Good hiking boots with a thick sole, preferably waterproof
- Socks, a clean pair for each day. I only use hiking socks, but my friend David uses white sports socks that he buys by the bundle, and he never gets blisters, so your choice.
- A kilt, a couple of pairs of trousers/shorts, your preference, but not jeans. Denim is one of the worst, most uncomfortable things to wear when wet. It is also constricting when you have to raise your leg when walking uphill or stepping over something.
- A change of underwear for each day and a change of clothing for dinner/drinks in the evening.

- T-shirt/shirt/sweatshirt, again your preference, but bear this in mind. When wet, cotton t-shirts are uncomfortable and you will get cold easily. If you are going for a t-shirt get them made from wick-away material these dry very quickly and are very comfortable. I would recommend that whatever clothes you are thinking about, consider layering your clothes, this is the best way to control your temperature. A wick-away t-shirt, a fleece and a waterproof jacket are my choice, and you can wear them in different configurations.
- Depending on time of year gloves may be needed, a hat is always a good idea. Unless it's winter (wool hat) and really cold, I always take a baseball cap, it can keep the sun out of your eyes and if it's raining it will keep the rain out of your face.
- A small day rucksack to carry water, lunch/snacks, camera, blister/first aid kit. This is only required if you are porting on your stuff and don't have your full size rucksack on your back.
- If you wish you could use a hiking pole, I have one and I can't say that I love or hate it. I tend to take it with me on the off chance I get attacked by a dog, to fend it off. After decades of hiking I have never been attacked.

Camping

- Over and above what is needed to stay in a hotel, you will need a tent, a sleeping mat, a sleeping bag (inside a plastic bag), your additional clothing should be in a plastic bag as well, I would suggest a clear one so you can see everything, much easier than emptying everything out.
- You may need a stove and food, your choice, food can be bought on these hikes.
- Toiletries, a flashlight/torch, toilet paper, bug spray (I would advise that when you have your tent up, spray the bug spray inside and close the tent while you go for dinner and a beer. That should deal with any midgies.

Weather

The weather will be, what it will be, and it's Scotland, so it can change hour by hour. So the only thing you can do is take clothing that you can layer on or off and take full waterproofs.

Informative websites

Currency converter
www.xe.com

Old roads of Scotland
www.oldroadsofscotland.com/military_roads.htm

The Doric Columns (The Drovers)
www.mcjazz.f2s.com/Drovers.htm

The West Highland Way
www.westhighlandway.org

VeryWellFit
The 8 Best Blister-Preventing Lubricants to Buy in 2018

By Wendy Bumgardner
www.verywellfit.com

Bibliography

With thanks to the following sources;

Mountain craft and Leadership

Eric Langmuir

On Location
(The film fans guide to Britain and Ireland)
Brian Pendreigh

The Munros
Donald Bennet

Scotland Coast to coast
Hamish Brown

Rucksack Readers
Handy guides

Footprint maps
Concise, easy guides

Biography

Paul Bissett was born in Edinburgh, Scotland and raised in the village of Blackness on the river Forth. At the age of seventeen he embarked upon a twenty-three-year career in the British Royal Navy, which took him all over the world. He has lived and worked in seven different countries.
He has, at various times been; a mountain guide; made and installed kilns in Australia; an instructor in Saudi Arabia; a Documentation Manager for a software company in Taiwan; and in the USA been a salesman for Sears, a firefighter, an Emergency Medical Technician (EMT), a jewelry store manager, and for the last twelve years, the senior case manager for the National Expert Witness Network based in Paradise, California.

Outside of work, he conducts Celtic and Scottish weddings. Hosts whiskey tastings, in California, Nevada and Oregon.

For fun, he researches whisky bars, writes/edits a whisky newsletter that goes out to readers in ten different countries.

He has written 2 books on hiking in the Scottish mountains and one on Whisky bars.

He also gives talks on all things Scottish, and has been the Master of Ceremonies at many events all over the world, including the Las Vegas Celtic Games (twice).
He currently lives in Yuba City, California, with his wife Tracey and their three dogs, Heather, Hamish and Luna.

My email is; paulwbissett@outlook.com

My website is; www.scot-talks.com

June
1 – Milngavie
(S)   Travelodge
       Dumbarton   £57.00

2 – Drymen Kip in the Kirk
(S)   £30.00
       Hill View

3 – Rowardennan   N.T.S.
(M)   £66.00

4. Inverarnan – Drover's Inn
(T)   £110.00

5. Tyndrum Hostel
(W)

39662503R00054

Printed in Poland
by Amazon Fulfillment
Poland Sp. z o.o., Wrocław